In the 191-year history of the United States Supreme Court, 101 men
have been appointed. In 1981 Sandra Day O'Connor was the
first woman appointed to the court.

SANDRA DAY O'CONNOR

First Woman on the Supreme Court

By Carol Greene

 CHILDRENS PRESS, CHICAGO

PHOTO CREDITS
Wide World Photos—2, 6, 15, 16–17, 24 (bottom), 26, 27, 31
Len Meents—8, 9, 10, 12
Black Star—Steve Northrup, 18
The Arizona Republic—20, 23, 24 (top)
Picture Group—© Nancy Engebretson, 22
The White House—Michael Evans, 28;
Mary Anne Fackelman, 29;
Bill Fitz-Patrick, 30

For Jordan Elizabeth Cooper

Library of Congress Cataloging in Publication Data

Greene, Carol.
  Sandra Day O'Connor.

  Summary: Traces the life of the first woman
appointed an associate justice of the highest
court in the country.
  1. O'Connor, Sandra Day, 1930-   —Juvenile
literature. 2. Judges—United States—
Biography—Juvenile literature. [1. O'Connor,
Sandra Day, 1930-   . 2. Judges. 3. United
States. Supreme Court—Biography] I. Title.
KF8745.025G73   347.73′2634 [B] 81-18038
                   347.3073534 [B] [92]
ISBN 0-516-06318-1   AACR2

1 2 3 4 5 6 7 8 9 10 R 91 90 89 88 87 86 85 84 83 82

SANDRA DAY O'CONNOR

First Woman on the Supreme Court

It feels great to be first. You know that feeling. So does Sandra Day O'Connor. She is the first woman to serve as a United States Supreme Court Justice.

President Ronald Reagan chose her for this job. But the Senate had to talk with her, too. They said "yes" by a vote of 99-0. On September 25, 1981, Sandra Day O'Connor was sworn into her new job. Someone asked her how she felt.

"Just great," she said.

Lazy B ranch

Sandra grew up on a ranch on
the border between Arizona and
New Mexico. Her grandfather,
Henry Day, had come from
Vermont in 1880 to start the ranch.
It didn't look like much back
then—just a lot of dust and cactus.
Henry Day bought 5,000 head of
cattle from Mexico. They were all
branded with a B. So he called his
ranch the Lazy B.

Ada Mae and Harry Day,
the proud parents of
Sandra Day O'Connor

When Henry Day died, his son
Harry took over the ranch. Harry
was Sandra's father. He met
Sandra's mother, Ada Mae, soon
after he came back to the ranch.
They were married and three years
later, in 1930, Sandra was born.

Sandra on her horse, Chico

Sandra's mother was her first
teacher. She ordered lessons by
mail and taught Sandra at home.
Sandra was only four then. She
worked hard at her lessons and she
loved to hear her mother read to
her. She also loved to ride her
horse, Chico. Her father taught her
to ride him when she was just three.

When Sandra was ready for first grade, she had to leave home. Her parents wanted her to go to a good school. But there weren't any good schools near the ranch. So Sandra went to live with her grandmother in El Paso, Texas. There she went to the Radford School for girls.

Every summer Sandra went back to the ranch. Those summers were great.

Ada Mae, Alan, Ann and Sandra Day

Sandra swam in the tank where water was stored. She learned how to brand cattle, mend fences, and even ride in roundups. When she was eight, her father taught her how to drive a truck and a tractor. And, sometimes, she played with dolls. By the time Sandra was ten, she had a brother, Alan, and a sister, Ann, to play with, too.

Sandra never wanted those summers to end. She'd always hide when it was time to go back to school. Once she and a friend got into the water tank and wouldn't come out. Her father had to rope them and pull them out!

But Sandra liked school once she got back. She had lots of plans and dreams about what she wanted to do when she grew up. Her parents thought her plans were wonderful. They believed Sandra could make them come true.

Sandra graduated from high school in El Paso when she was sixteen years old. Then she went to Stanford University. In only five years she finished all the courses she had to take to be a lawyer. She graduated *magna cum laude* (that means "with great distinction"). She was the third highest person in her law school class.

1948

1950

1950

1950

Sandra went to Stanford University in California. In 1950 she
was elected president of the senior class.

In 1952 Sandra Day (second from left in third row) posed with her law school classmates at Stanford University.

Then Sandra looked for a job. She talked to law firms in Los Angeles and San Francisco. None of them would give her a job.

"We've never hired a woman lawyer before," they said. "And we don't want to do it now."

Finally one group of lawyers
said, "You can be our secretary."

But Sandra said, "No." She had
her plans and dreams and she
wasn't going to give them up. She
had studied to be a lawyer and
that's what she was going to be.

John Jay O'Connor III (left) married Sandra Day in 1952.

First, though, she married a
man she had met in law school,
John Jay O'Connor III. John still
had to finish law school, so while
he did Sandra got a job as a deputy
county attorney in San Mateo,
California. Then they both worked
as lawyers in Frankfurt, West
Germany, for three years.

In 1957 the O'Connors moved to
Phoenix, Arizona. Their first son,
Scott, was born there. Later they
had two more sons, Brian and Jay.

For a while Sandra had her own
law office. Then she decided to be a
full-time homemaker. She took
care of her husband, the children,
and their home. She was president
of the Junior League, a club for
women, and joined other clubs, too.
She helped the Salvation Army.
She worked for free at a school for
black and Hispanic children.
Sandra was a very busy woman!

Sandra taking oath of office when she became a state senator.

Finally she decided she was doing just too many things. It would make more sense for her to go back to a regular job. So for four years she worked as an assistant attorney general in Arizona. Then she became a state senator.

Meanwhile, more and more people were learning what a good worker Sandra was. She understood exactly what each law meant and she could explain it to others. She could look at a law and tell what was wrong with it. Then she could make it right.

Sandra wearing her judicial robe.

More important, Sandra
O'Connor was fair. She didn't care
if people liked her or not. She just
wanted to do the right thing. And
she worked hard to find out what
the right thing was.

A fellow Arizona judge greets Sandra.

People did like her because she *was* so fair and worked so hard. She could have become a famous politician. But deep down, Sandra loved law more than politics. So she ran in an election for judge—and won. Now she was a judge for the Maricopa County Superior Court in Arizona.

Above: John Jay O'Connor helps Sandra on with her judicial robe in 1979.
Later Sandra posed with her fellow judges on the Arizona Court of Appeals (below).

Once again people could see how fair Sandra O'Connor was. She wouldn't let anybody get away with anything. She always did exactly what the law said. Sometimes she didn't *like* what the law said, but she did it anyway.

Before long, Bruce Babbitt, the governor of Arizona, asked Sandra to be a judge on the Arizona Court of Appeals. That was a very important job. She kept it until President Reagan chose her for something even more important— the U.S. Supreme Court.

Scott O'Connor (above) kisses his mother at a news conference she held
after President Reagan nominated her for the United States Supreme
Court. Right: Sandra poses with her family (from left to right:
sons Brian, Scott, Jay and husband John).

Sandra O'Connor and her
husband now live in a beautiful
home in Paradise Valley. It is only
225 miles away from the Lazy B
ranch where her parents still live.
Her sons, Scott, Brian, and Jay,
spent their summers on the ranch
when they were growing up just as
their mother did. And everyone in
the family still goes back often for
visits.

President Ronald Reagan (middle) and one of his advisors (left)
share a joke with Sandra during a White House talk.

When she isn't working, Sandra
likes to play golf and tennis, dance,
listen to country music, cook
Mexican food, and—of course—ride
horses. She told President Reagan
that she thought the best place in
the world to be was on a horse out
with the cattle. He probably
agreed!

President Ronald Reagan, Chief Justice Warren Burger, and Associate
Justice Sandra Day O'Connor.

The Supreme Court is the
highest court in the United States.
It helps other courts understand
laws and how they work. Supreme
Court Justices keep their jobs until
they die or resign. Justice Sandra
O'Connor now has the most
important U. S. government job
any woman ever has had.

The Supreme Court of the United States in 1981—(from left to right: Associate Justices Harry A. Blackmun, Thurgood Marshall, William A. Brennan, Chief Justice Warren E. Burger, Associate Justices Sandra D. O'Connor, Bryon R. White, Lewis F. Powell, William H. Rehnquist, John P. Stevens).

But Sandra O'Connor is important for another reason, too. She's important because she never let people stop her from making her dreams and plans come true. She *knew* a woman could be a good lawyer and a good judge and she proved it. Other girls and women can look at her and feel better about making their own dreams and plans come true.

Sandra Day O'Connor and Chief Justice of the Supreme Court Warren E. Burger

People used to call the men on
the Supreme Court "the Brethren."
("Brethren" means "brothers.")
That name doesn't work anymore.
Now the Brethren have a
sister—Sandra Day O'Connor.

Sandra Day O'Connor

1930	March 26—Born in El Paso, Texas, the first child of Harry and Ada Mae Day
1950	Graduated from Stanford University, Stanford, California
1952	Graduated from Stanford University's School of Law
1952	Married John Jay O'Connor III
1952	Became a deputy county attorney in San Mateo, California
1954–57	Worked as a civilian lawyer for the United States Army in Frankfurt, West Germany
1959	Began her own law business in Phoenix, Arizona
1965–69	Worked as an assistant attorney general
1969–74	Served as an Arizona state senator
1974–79	Served as an Arizona Superior Court judge for Maricopa County
1979–81	Served as a judge for the Arizona Court of Appeals
1981	July 7—Named by President Ronald Reagan to the Supreme Court
1981	September 25—Took oath of office as a United States Supreme Court Justice

About the Author

CAROL GREENE has written over 20 books for children, plus stories, poems, songs, and filmstrips. She has also worked as a children's editor and a teacher of writing for children. She received a B. A. in English Literature from Park College, Parkville, Missouri, and an M. A. in Musicology from Indiana University. Ms. Greene lives in St. Louis, Missouri. When she isn't writing, she likes to read, travel, sing, do volunteer work at her church—and write some more. Her *The Super Snoops and the Missing Sleepers* has also been published by Childrens Press.